The Victorian Scrap Gallery

The Victorian Scrap Gallery

A Collection of Over
500 Full-Color
Victorian-Era Images

**Dee Davis and
Gail B. Cooper**

Watson-Guptill Publications / New York

Acknowledgments

We would like to thank:

Our dear friend and artist, Christopher Burton of Odgen, Utah, who shares our interests in decoupage, collecting paper ephemera, and wonderful food. It was through his thoughtfulness that we were able to obtain Laura's scrapbooks.

The multitalented Milton Cooper for once again unselfishly sharing his experience, advice, and magical graphic skills. His touch added greatly to the beauty and quality of this book.

Stephen Cooper for his patient organizing, reorganizing, and editing during our research and writing about the history of printed scrap, and for contributing his rather amazing knowledge of nineteenth-century popular culture.

Our "gallery" team, who have worked with us this second time around: Joy Aquilino, our editor, of blessed disposition; it's always a pleasure to work with her, and Areta Buk, our art director, whose creativity and taste we treasure.

Scrapbook artist and author Jill Miller, for the generous contribution of her time and talent. The scrapbook page and gift tags she created for this book (see pages 21 and 24) are beautiful examples of how Victorian scrap can enhance paper projects.

Dee would also like to thank:

My children, Laurie Gilkes and Peter Davis, for their constant love, support, and encouragement, and my grandchildren, Amy Gilkes and Conner Davis, for all the wonderful times together with love and laughter and artwork.

Gail would also like to thank:

Warren, for staying the same and being there, Linda, for teaching me more than she realizes; Burt for the guest room and all the Kodachrome; Richard and Susan for being here and always showing up; my son, Stephen, and my husband, Milton, for all their hard work and for being remarkably good sports.

Senior Aquisition Editor: Joy Aquilino
Edited by Laaren Brown
Graphic production by Hector Campbell
Text set in Adobe Garamond

Front cover, clockwise from upper left: The chinoiserie theme of the scrap works harmoniously with the Asian-calligraphy wrapping paper. The large bouquet fits perfectly on this garden journal. A single pink flower and tropical blue painted background turn a small glass dish into a charming candy holder. A Victorian collage of greeting cards and scrap encircles a special valentine on the memory box.

Previous spread, clockwise from lower left: For this elegant Asian fan, we paired similar (but not identical) figures on coffee-tinted background paper; the fan is covered in orange silk shantung with black-and-orange silk cord edging. The black tray, top left, uses compatible flowers from several prints. On the octagonal plate, the apricot color chosen for the painted background repeats the apricot accents on the flower. The tiger coaster and greeting card show how the same image (reversed) can be used with different backgrounds to produce very different results.

Contents

Introduction

Once upon a time in the Midwestern United States, in the year 1887, a baby girl was born to a young couple recently arrived from Denmark. They named her Laura.

The family enjoyed a typical Victorian-era lifestyle. Their spare time was spent together, going to church, gardening, caring for pets, crafting, and sewing. And as a youngster, Laura Friese was absorbed with the current craze for scrapbooking.

One hundred years later, we were able to acquire Laura's scrapbooks, which had been carefully preserved by her daughter, Dorothea. On the front page of each book, in childlike script, is written "Laura A. Friese 1897." The images from Laura's books are beautiful and in perfect condition.

This charming card, from Laura's scrapbook, was one of many exchanged by members of the family.

The Victorian Scrap Gallery has been assembled from Laura's scrap, combined with images from our own collection.

The end of the twentieth century, the beginning of a new millennium, or perhaps simply the longing for what we perceive as a simpler, more romantic time has fueled a mania for vintage collectibles. Bygone pastimes such as keeping journals, diaries, and scrapbooks have once again become a craze. Victorian scrap images are one of the most charming and authentic ways to enhance these projects.

We wish you a most wonderful time using them, now and happily ever after.

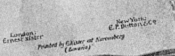

The History of Victorian Scrap

Small elegant images, printed on fine-quality paper in rich colors, gloss coated, deeply embossed, and die cut, are referred to as scrap, printed scrap, Victorian scrap, or antique scrap. These charming images were extremely popular throughout the nineteenth century (dubbed the Victorian era, 1837 to 1901, after Queen

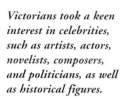

Victoria). Printed scrap, and the ways in which it reflects nineteenth-century popular culture, offers a rare glimpse into this remarkable time.

By the turn of the nineteenth century, the Industrial Revolution, economic progress, increase in

Victorians took a keen interest in celebrities, such as artists, actors, novelists, composers, and politicians, as well as historical figures.

free trade, and new educational opportunities had given rise to a literate middle class with a surplus of money to spend and a great deal of spare time to fill. This new bourgeoisie enthusiastically embraced the leisure activities popular among the upper class. Reading by the fireside, playing an instrument, engaging in a variety of craft arts now took hold among this large middle class.

One of the more popular hobbies was the collecting of black-and-white prints. The prints typically featured exotic plants and animals, or people and fashions from distant cities. The images would often be colored in by hand, then cut out and pasted onto decorative and useful objects—a pastime referred to by its French name, "découpage."

The prints were also pasted into diaries and journals, along with poems, decorative advertising tags, trade cards, and fancy product wrappings. Because most of the cutout images were small, they were commonly referred to as "scraps."

While black-and-white or single-color prints had existed for decades, the ability to print on paper in a multitude of colors wasn't developed until 1837, by a Frenchman, Godefroy Engelmann. Engelmann's contribution—a process of separating an image into four constituent colors, which could then be used to reproduce images in up to twenty-four colors—meant that full-color images could be produced. (This early color printing was called chromolithography, from the Greek "chroma," meaning color.)

Victorian scrap enthusiasts were thrilled with these color images and used them for decoupage and to enhance diaries, journals, and special albums manufactured expressly for collectors of the new colored prints.

As manufacturing technology progressed, printers developed processes that made scrap images much more attractive, such as a gloss coating that gave them a high shine. The printed sheets were then embossed—a process that raises areas of the image. (Embossed images were originally referred to as "embossed reliefs," because the raised surface resembled bas-relief.) The printed, gloss-coated, embossed sheets (sometimes they were even gilded) would then be die cut, a process that cuts away the background and leaves a shaped image. The die-cut images remained delicately attached to one another by thin paper strips known as "ladders"; just a snip was necessary to detach a ladder, and the image was ready to use—no intricate cutting needed. These new techniques turned the already popular hobby of scrap collecting into an absolute craze.

A completed sheet of scrap had multiples of the same print or related yet slightly different prints. These easy-to-use colored scraps were first used by bakers in Germany as decorations on holiday cakes and confirmation wafers. They quickly became sought after for use in decoupage, albums, and journals.

Images that appealed to the Victorians' interests were very popular: virtually every collector wanted the romantic themes of the time, sentimental pictures of women and children, cherubs, angels, flowers, and scenes from nature. Religious images and holiday themes, especially pictures related to Christmas, were also great favorites.

Objects would be totally covered in scrap images of various subjects and sizes, most pieces overlapping one another with very little background showing. Advertising cards, paper lace, and memorabilia were often added. And when printers in Germany began producing embossed and die-cut gold foil trims (often called Dresdens), it was used in abundance. Even ribbons, tassels, laces, and jewels were added, especially on cards and ornaments. The compositions appeared playfully cluttered, but worked harmoniously and had great charm. It is this type of composition that is referred to as "the Victorian look."

Increasingly elaborate scrap albums, many of which were leather bound with extravagantly embossed and gilded covers, brass

Victorians became fascinated with chinoiserie. Large numbers of scraps featuring interpretations of Asian culture were printed and widely collected.

American themes such as flags, famous Americans, and battle scenes were immensely popular. The American frontier was an especially fascinating subject, both in our country and in Europe, and many scraps were produced showing pictures of cowboys and Indians.

locks, and special endpapers, were produced. Some had pages of beautiful papers printed with decorative pictures or die-cut frames in which the scraps could be placed. The widespread demand for these materials even resulted in a new kind of store, the fancy stationery shop. Tiffany & Company, now famous for its jewelry, actually began as a fancy stationery store in the early 1800s.

Families would spend their evenings at home together, the floor covered with sheets of colored scraps, cards, and memorabilia, happily sorting and pasting materials into their books. Queen Victoria herself collected colored scrap images, as did her Master of the

Household, Lord Edward Clinton, whose own scrapbooks formed an extraordinary collection of royal memorabilia.

Scrap enthusiasts avidly collected scrap images commemorating special events. In 1840, when Queen Victoria married her cousin, Prince Albert of Saxe-Coburg-Gotha, beautiful embossed scraps were printed to celebrate the wedding. When Prince Albert organized the Great Exhibition of 1851, scraps appeared commemorating the event. Other scraps highlighted the technological achievements of the era.

Color printing reached its finest quality in the mid-nineteenth century in France and Germany. Germany, which had some of the most technically advanced printing

Not all scraps were small; they could vary in size from one inch high to as much as twelve inches high. This exquisitely printed scrap of a woman in a cream-and-burgundy outfit measures five by nine inches.

This Victorian valentine is a printed, embossed, die-cut card with paper lace and scrap pictures added.

plants, produced enormous quantities of scrap sheets at low prices. It is not unusual to see scrap published by a British or American company bearing a Printed in Germany tag.

The increasing demand for new images led to a seemingly endless amount of scrap art, which captured a wide variety of activities from middle- and upper-class Victorian life. Country scenes of fox hunting and farming, city scenes of horse-drawn vehicles, favorite sports such as boxing, badminton, cricket, and polo are all pictured in scrap.

The completion of the transatlantic cable was one of the great engineering feats of the nineteenth century.

When Commodore Matthew Perry established a new relationship between Japan and the Western world in 1854, there was a huge revival of interest in chinoiserie, resulting in exotic scrap featuring European adaptations of Asian motifs.

In midcentury scrap, new forms of transportation and the latest designs for textiles and furniture were reflected. Idealized Victorian families were shown visiting the zoo, attending the circus, and journeying to the seashore. These families were invariably composed of extremely sweet-looking ladies, distinguished gentleman, and charming children, all dressed in the richly colored fabrics of the latest fashions.

Elaborate Christmas and Valentine cards were introduced and also sold in great quantities. In fact, modern Valentine's Day cards are modeled after styles of the Victorian era. Cupid with his arrow, cherubs, and soft, creamy tones of pink, red, mauve, and gold are still traditional. Many Valentines were made from fluffy layers of elaborate lace paper, sometimes with gold or silver embossing. They were attached to printed, embossed cards, die-cut into beautiful shapes. Some even had mica sprinkled on them for a sparkly effect. The Victorians added

scrap to these cards. Oftentimes the added scraps would hold a small secret message or love poem, concealed by an illustration of a hand or other decorative element that was meant to be lifted in private.

By the latter part of the nineteenth century Victorian life had changed profoundly. Improvements in transportation, inventions such as telephones and telegraphs, and new amusements for leisure time combined with improved health and continued prosperity led people toward a new lifestyle. They began going out more, traveling, and seeking new things to do outside the home. It is little wonder that the home-based activity of collecting and using scraps waned with the approach of the twentieth century.

Ultimately, the elegant, beautiful scrapbooks, albums, journals, and decoupage pieces were put away in attics and trunks, where they gathered dust along with other relics of

Even Santa used a new mode of transportation.

the Victorian era. And yet these images have an enduring appeal, as does so much of the aesthetics of the Victorian era. Perhaps, as you look through these pages, you may, for a few moments, step into the nineteenth century, imagine the faint perfume of lavender hanging in the air, and daydream of times past.

Scrap from the late nineteenth century featured many of the latest inventions.

My dear Sweetheart

Essential Techniques

With your heart and your hands—plus these simple instructions—you will soon be creating scrapbooks, greeting cards, valentines, gift wraps, collages, even heirloom pieces of decoupage. The enchanting scrap pictures in the gallery will combine harmoniously with your photographs, newspaper clippings, and all your other special memorabilia.

❖

Clockwise from lower left: Cats are grouped around a central trio on this decorative plate. Angels on the frame above fly around flowers, giving action to the composition. Trims and other elements enhance greeting cards. Use neutral backgrounds for gift items such as this dog tray. Using only one subject—roses—makes the red heart box a modern adaptation of Victorian-style collage. The round valentine box was painted in the blue-gray accent color of the print.

To My Little Sweetheart

Working with Prints and Papers

Papers come in many weights and qualities. Thicker paper makes fine, detailed cutting difficult, is harder to glue, and requires multiple varnish coats to cover. Thinner paper can wrinkle when gluing and the background color of the surface might show through the image; any printing on the back of the paper might also show through.

Printing inks can fade over time, affected by sunlight and artificial light. The inks in this book won't run, but many papers "bleed" if dampened. So test with a bit of wet paper towel before using. A word of warning: Most gift wrap is not acid-free and it will not last; the inks will fade with time.

Laser photocopies are the solution to several of these problems. We have found laser-copy paper easy to cut and glue, there is no print on the back, and the inks do not run when dampened. Additionally, color photocopy machines can enlarge or reduce images, enhance or mute colors, make reverse (mirror) images, and even repeat images in multiples across a page. You can preserve your original documents, invitations, and vintage photos by making copies as needed. (Note that you may copy anything for your personal use, but check copyright laws if you are selling your work.)

To create an antique look, copy on off-white paper. To age the paper yourself, lightly coat the paper with cold black

coffee or tea using a clean sponge or a brush. Blot up any puddles and let dry.

The colors of most prints can be touched up with artists' oil pencils, available in a wide range of colors at art supply stores (brands include Derwent and Prismacolor). Use these pencils for coloring the edges of cut images and also for thickening fine lines before cutting. If you are using markers, be sure they specify permanent; some are available with permanent acid-free inks. We used markers for names and borders on some of the decoupaged bars of soap. Often we sign and date our work with silver or gold markers.

Original images of die-cut scrap were held together by thin paper strips called "ladders." You'll notice that we left ladders on some of the scrap. You, too, can use this trick on a print. Pencil in ladders (before cutting) to support an arm, antennae, or leaf that is attached in only one place. Draw a double pencil line from the tip of the leaf to the nearest object in the picture. Cut out around the ladders, but remember to trim them off just before gluing.

The dotted lines indicate the penciled-in ladders; cut around them as if they were part of the image. Ladders keep delicate details from breaking off.

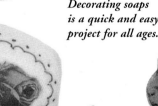

Decorating soaps is a quick and easy project for all ages.

Sealing

Always seal prints and papers. Acrylic sealer protects the paper and inks from damage and strengthens the paper. Seal the front of the image before cutting or gluing unless you are gluing under glass; if you are putting the picture under glass, seal the *back* of the paper. When working with large pieces of paper, sealing both the front and the back will make it easier to handle the picture and to glue without wrinkles.

Acrylic sealer is available in spray cans in art supply stores. Spray two or three light coats; let dry five minutes between coats. Unfortunately this spray sealer is toxic; use it outdoors or in a well-ventilated space. We recommend liquid brush-on acrylic sealer as an alternative. It is water-based and nontoxic but harder to find. The search for it is worthwhile, because it seals not only paper but also porous and painted surfaces. Paper needs only one coat of brush-on sealer. Let dry about twenty minutes before cutting.

The photocopy in this Victorian frame was aged with coffee. The dark background color adds drama.

Paper crafters should use acid-free or archival products whenever possible. Acid-free materials will not react with chemicals in photos and mementos, and therefore will not cause untimely deterioration; they will last a very long time. Archival materials are chemically balanced, so they are durable and will last even longer than acid-free materials, but there is no standard for exactly how much longer. Professional conservators always use archival materials.

Scissors Art

To stay on the cutting edge, you need curved cuticle scissors with narrow, sharp blades. Straight scissors cut the straightest lines, and curved scissors cut the smoothest curves (which is almost everything you'll be cutting). The best-quality scissors are made of Soligen steel, which stays sharp the longest time. Never use your papercraft scissors for anything that might dull the blades, even a cuticle.

With practice, some people can cut skillfully with a craft knife, a scalpel, even a single-edge razor blade. Cutting on a pane of glass or a cutting mat helps keep the blade sharp.

Paper-edger scissors finish the straight edges of paper prints, cards, or photos in a decorative way. With different edgers, you can deckle, serrate, and scallop edges quickly and easily, transforming artwork from plain to fancy.

Cutting

Practice the following cutting technique on some throw-away magazine pictures until you feel comfortable with it. Pick up the scissors with the right thumb and middle finger, supported underneath by the index finger. Always check that the curved blades are pointing to the *right,* facing away from the paper. The left hand holds the paper loosely, turning it around and back, feeding it to the scissors. The right hand stays in position, smoothly opening and closing the scissors in a steady rhythm. If you are left-handed, reverse the above instructions (although we have known some lefties who prefer cutting right-handed).

The point of using this technique is that you can see exactly *where* you are cutting, so you can cut more accurately. If your cutouts are outlined by background paper, cut closer to the edge of the image; it won't hurt if you cut away a sliver of the print. Sharp scissors will cut crisply; clutching them will only make your fingers sore. Relax, sit comfortably. With good light, you won't tire your eyes; a

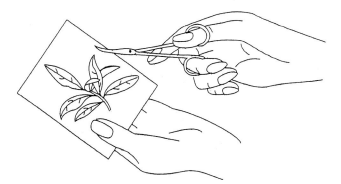

Hold the paper in your left hand and the scissors in your right hand, pointing away from the paper. This way you can see exactly where the blades are cutting.

towel in your lap will catch most of the cuttings, and soothing music will make your pastime even more enjoyable. Start by cutting simple images, then progress to more intricate things. Really fine cutting takes a lot of practice. Enjoy discovering the fascinating things you can do with scissors and paper.

Smaller pieces of paper are easier to handle; three to five inches is a good size. Begin by cutting away empty sections of background paper. You do not need to use the entire picture; you can use just one section, keeping the rest for another occasion. A very large print can even be cut apart into smaller sections at strategic points, the images cut out, and the whole glued back together without showing the joins.

Before you cut around the outer edges of the print, remove the small interior sections of plain background. Poke a small hole in the center of each interior section, then put the scissors underneath the paper, poke the tips up through the hole, and cut away all the blank paper.

Cutting the interior, removing some background, and refining the foliage details sharpens the focus on the leopard.

A craft knife with a small tip is helpful for very small interior areas. Trimming away these sections takes a bit of practice, but it is worth it. The final image will have more depth and look more realistic. If you forget to cut out a small area, you can always fill it in with a coloring pencil or dot of paint that matches the background.

After you have completely finished cutting out some images, lay them out face up on a dark surface. If you don't see any traces of background paper, you are doing great. Now turn your cutouts over, facedown, and see if you can tell what the object is by looking at the silhouette. If not,

To make a matching bud or a smaller bloom, cut away the outer petals of a larger flower.

study the picture to figure out how to improve the shape by cutting more and refining details. Be brave! It's only practice paper, and there's plenty more.

You will be amazed to discover all the tricks you can do with a scissors. Is that flower too big? Cut away some of the outer petals...then add them to another flower that's too small. Want texture for leaves or fur or feathers? Practice serrated cutting to produce an edge like a serrated knife. Use your left hand to turn and wiggle the paper back and forth as you cut with your right hand. Small zigzags make sharp serrations; larger movements make a softer scalloped edge. With a bit of practice, you will be delighted by the results.

When making scrapbooks, cards, or anything using photos, try cropping and reshaping the picture. Using plastic templates, you can change the shape to a circle, oval, triangular, or hexagon vignette. Place the template over the picture until you get just the part you want. Outline the template with a pencil, then cut the shape out. Frame it with a cartouche of flowers or enclose it with a colorful border. Outline the edge with paint or marker or cut with paper-edgers if you like.

If you want the butterfly to rest on a flower, cut away one half and place the other half on the blossom. The wings will appear to be folded.

Serrated cutting creates a more realistic texture for the bear's fur. Slightly exaggerating the serration of the leaf shows nature's details.

Using plastic templates, we cut these vignettes from images in the gallery.

Scrap was combined with decorative paper to create this plate. Decorative papers work well for backgrounds, mats, or frames when they harmonize with the pictures. Add interest by combining them with the scrap.

Preparing Surfaces for Decoration

As you know, the surface should be clean and free of dust, dry and smooth. You must seal all porous surfaces so that paint and glue will not be absorbed into the surface but will bond properly. Here are some specifics on preparing various surfaces.

Paper: Protect paper backgrounds and images for scrapbook pages, greeting cards, gift wrap, and everything else with sealer before gluing.

Wood: Denatured alcohol will remove grime and grease on old wood objects. Repair cracks and dents with wood filler and let dry thoroughly. Then sand the wood smooth, working with the grain, and wipe off the dust with a tack cloth before sealing. New pieces of wood may also need a little sanding; when finished, wipe clean with a tack cloth, seal, and let dry. If you are using wood primer, follow the manufacturer's instructions.

Tin: Old pieces should be cleaned of grease and grime by wiping with denatured alcohol. Old painted pieces may need sanding to remove all rust and flaking paint. After sanding, wash the metal clean and dry it thoroughly. Then seal or prepare with metal primer, following the manufacturer's directions.

Glass: Clean with soap, then rinse, putting a few drops of ammonia in the rinse water. Dry thoroughly, using a chamois for a lint-free surface. If you are gluing under glass, it is not necessary to seal the surface of the glass; instead, you will need to seal the back, not the front, of the image.

Soap or candles: Waxy surfaces first need a coat of acrylic medium. Let dry, then glue the scrap with the medium for best adhesion. Coat only the top surface of the bar of soap (so that later the soap can be used from the bottom) and let dry. Protect the decorated top of the bar with either two coats of the medium or with acrylic finish.

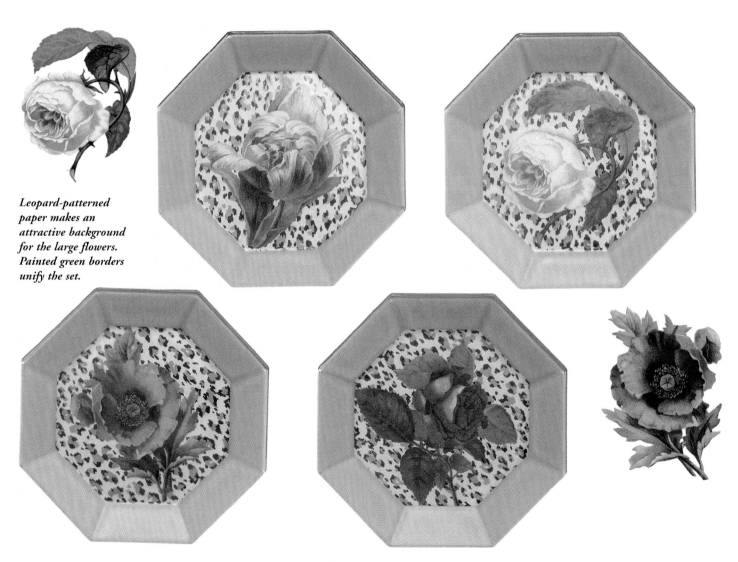

Leopard-patterned paper makes an attractive background for the large flowers. Painted green borders unify the set.

Basic Technique for Coating Any Wood, Tin, or Ceramic Surface with Sealer, Paint, or Finish

1. Clean surface, using a tack cloth, before each coat.

2. Have a container of water handy to moisten your brush, thin paint, and clean up.

3. Moisten sponge brush (polybrush). The sponge should be only slightly damp.

4. Pour out as much sealer, paint, or finish as you will need into a small plastic container and close the original jar or tin tightly.

5. Dip brush halfway into the sealer, paint, or finish, and start your stroke in the center of the surface, working toward the edge. Load brush according to size of surface, lightly for small, more heavily for larger areas.

6. Hold brush at a forty-five-degree angle. Flow; don't drag; use light pressure. (Pressing hard makes bubbles.)

7. Keep your surface horizontal. Liquids will run down a vertical surface.

8. Start each loaded brush on a dry area, working your way back into the wet area. Brush with parallel strokes.

9. Prop up object to air dry. Clean brush in warm soapy water.

10. Allow sufficient drying time. The drying time of all liquids depends on the thickness of the application. High humidity or cold temperatures will slow drying.

Color Choices

The color of your piece should enhance and harmonize with your images. Spread out an assortment of colored papers (tissue, construction, whatever). Lay out your images on these different colors and select the one that looks the best with your prints.

If you are using a paper background, carefully choose patterned or textured papers that are appropriate and will not detract from the theme of the scrap and memorabilia.

For a traditional period piece, use the colors of that particular period. A contemporary style allows a wider range of bold colors. Dark, strong colors are dramatic, but be careful of the intensity; the background should enhance, not dominate. Neutral colors are always safe, particularly if you will be selling the final piece or giving it as a present. That gift you hope will grace your friend's living room might just end up in a drawer if it is flamingo pink.

You can't go wrong choosing a background color that is an accent (small amount) color in your images. If you want to use a color that is dominant in your prints, try using a shade of it that is either darker or lighter.

Latex paints and acrylic paints are water-based, fast-drying, and odor-free. Any of the available sheens are acceptable except gloss, which repels glue and topcoat. If you are unsure about a color choice, first make a sample, let it dry, and then look at your prints with the color. That's easier than repainting the whole surface.

Usually two or three coats of paint provide good coverage, although some transparent colors might need more. Always allow sufficient drying time (up to five hours) between coats or the paint might crack later on. If necessary, lightly sand between coats of paint with a medium or fine sanding pad. It takes practice to produce a smooth, even coating. Seal the painted surface when dry. This will protect it from damage as you place and glue prints.

Painting on Glass or Plastic

Pat on the paint with a cosmetic sponge to avoid brushstrokes. Apply *thin* coats of paint to let all the moisture evaporate. For glass, first pat on a thin coat of acrylic medium, which gives a better bond, and let dry before painting.

For most crafts purposes, brush-on paint, sealer, or finish works better than spray cans. Spray cans make it more difficult to get smooth, even coverage without drips and runs, and it usually takes several spray coats to equal one brush-on coat. However, spraying gives the best coverage for heavily carved surfaces and woven baskets.

As you experiment, you will discover that some plastic-coated or slick, glossy surfaces repel almost every glue and coating. If glued papers lift off in a few days, wrap the entire decorated surface with clear Mylar, a polyester archival material.

Planning and Composition

Organize your memorabilia, images, and photos by category and then place them in plastic sheet protectors, plastic zipper bags, manila envelopes, or archival boxes. Label each with year, occasion, person, theme, or category. As you begin a project, look through everything you have and start to put images together. Try any and all ideas that pop into your head. Forget your inhibitions and experiment. Everyone can be creative. Just give yourself a chance. The more you do, the more ideas you will get and the easier it all becomes. There isn't any right or wrong—just good, better, and best. Trust your eye to select the best. Serious or humorous, traditional or contemporary...it's up to you.

After you cut away backgrounds from prints, you won't have as much material as it first seemed. It is better to have too much to select from than too little. Even if you have cut out more flowers than you are using, just store the extras away flat in a plastic bag. They won't fade and will be ready for another project.

If your project has a flat surface, practice composing on a paper pattern cut to that size. The layout for your scrapbook, card, or other project can capture a memory, tell a story, or relate to a theme. Try cutting several paper patterns, and experiment with a variety of choices. Illustrate your theme by combining scrap, photos, ephemera, and perhaps a color-coordinated border.

If your choice is a three-dimensional object (such as a box), compose directly on the object. Attach the cutouts to the sealed surface with bits of removable adhesive such as Hold It, masking tape, or removable Scotch tape.

Whether you are working on a flat surface or a three-dimensional object, start by placing the largest and most important images. These are the focus of the composition. Next, place the smaller coordinating pieces.

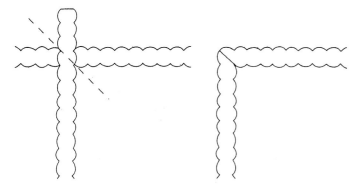

To create a frame using a border, mitre the corners by cutting through the two overlapping pieces on a diagonal at each corner. Remove excess, then glue pieces in place.

The curve is the line of beauty. Place your images on an imaginary curve. Whenever possible, have the action going into and around the theme, like arrows pointing the way. This brings the viewer's eye into the picture.

Combine images in a variety of sizes and shapes. Place a small flower next to the larger one; try it above, below, or tilt it at a different angle. If you are pairing images to create balance, add interest by choosing similar pieces rather than identical ones. Variations in subject matter and shades of a color are more interesting visually. Group several images together to create a focus and place the others at different levels, around the group. Uneven numbers—three, five, seven—of images will make the composition more dynamic. Experiment with off-center placement, which can be more dramatic than centered.

There are many lovely borders here to complement the scrap. As you compose, try some and you'll see how decorative they can be, enhancing a picture and directing focus to the overall theme. When you want to make something quick and easy, just use a whole print by itself. Choose the shape and color of the object carefully, so it will be striking though simple. You can have great fun taking inspiration for your own compositions from the layered Victorian style, a forerunner of collage.

Collage (from the French *coller,* to glue) is a process of selecting and assembling a variety of materials including fabrics, cutouts, and three-dimensional objects. It makes good use of overlapping layers of these assorted images and textures.

Decoupage (from the French *découper,* to cut up), by contrast, is more concerned with the fine cutting and creative composition of paper images. Traditionally, the cut pieces are "redesigned," matched like a jigsaw puzzle and glued in place so well that no one can tell where they separate.

As you work on your composition, check how it looks up close and also from a distance. Place the object on a plastic turntable (a lazy susan) and slowly rotate it at arm's length, checking the rhythm and flow of shapes and colors. Does the design lead your eye into and around the object? Do those spaces need some minor adjustment? If so, lift the cutout and hold it with long tweezers, moving it around until your eye tells you "Just right!" Keep on turning, looking and changing until you are satisfied.

Before gluing, put your project in its proper place: the wastebasket on the floor, the frame on the wall. You may discover that you need to make adjustments due to both distance and eye level.

Don't get discouraged. Often it is better to take a break and return refreshed later. Sometimes it is the size or shape of the object that makes the composition difficult. Try placing the images on something else or in another way. For example, notice that some of these pages of Victorian scrap are horizontal, and some are vertical. As we composed the coordinating images around the larger ones, sometimes with borders, we arranged and rearranged to find the best compositions, trying to use as many images as possible while leaving enough space around each for you to cut it out easily.

When you are satisfied with your composition, mark the placement of each cutout. On paper, make light pencil marks *under* the image, putting small dots at top, bottom, and sides. On a washable surface (where you can wipe off your marks), use a piece of colored chalk to outline cutouts. On glass, mark the outside of the glass with a grease pencil. Check borders with a T-square or ruler to be sure they are straight.

If all this is new to you, you cannot absorb it in one reading. If you are having problems, it could be helpful to reread these directions once in a while. Soon, these ideas will come to you automatically as you work. There are literally hundreds of different roads an artist can take. Feel free to change your mind and keep designing until you are really happy with your composition and can't wait to glue. Enjoy the creative process and, like the Victorians, have a good time with your pastime!

With the background color showing, the stool becomes a contemporary interpretation of Victorian-style collage. We couldn't resist adding tassels as a finishing touch.

19

Glues and Gluing

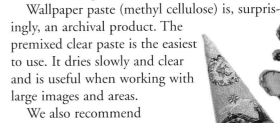

This is a very sticky subject that can lead to a lot of confusion. Sorry about that pun! Although there are many glues on the market, all you need is a small assortment, depending on the background surface you are using.

Gluing paper to paper: Scrapbook pages, greeting cards, and any paper surfaces are porous and cannot be safely cleaned of excess glue even after sealing. Use a very small amount of adhesive so that it won't spread past the edges of the images.

There are many acid-free types of glue on the market. They come as solid sticks, gels, and liquids; all are easy to apply and dry clear. Several liquid glues come in felt-tip-pen-style applicators. Some glues allow more time to reposition your images than others. Experiment with sample papers and different glues to decide which you prefer. Our favorites are Yasumoto Glue-It Pen, Elmer's No-Wrinkle Glue Pen, and Ross Rubber Cement, a new product marked no-wrinkle, acid-free. We tried this recently, and found it works just like older rubber cement products, which are not acid-free.

Double-stick tape is handy for attaching heavier paper and photos. Use a ruler to guide the straight-line placement.

Gluing paper to wood, tin, and glass: For a rigid surface that can be cleaned, like wood or glass, use a water-soluble, nontoxic adhesive, either white glue or acrylic medium. On average, white glue dries in ten to thirty minutes and acrylic medium in thirty to forty-five minutes.

Both dry clear and are easiest to remove while wet. Some of the new gel glues can also be used on these materials. Read labels carefully and test on your surface.

White PVA glue, made by Elmer's and Sobo, bonds paper to most surfaces, except plastic. Be sure to clean off any excess glue as it shows up very shiny when dry. PVA glue is considered an archival product.

Acrylic medium (matte) and Mod Podge (matte) work well for bonding paper to glass or plastic and for gluing thin papers and larger prints. If the medium is too runny, pour some out into a saucer and it will thicken as the moisture evaporates. (This is a useful trick for almost any water-based liquid.)

Wallpaper paste (methyl cellulose) is, surprisingly, an archival product. The premixed clear paste is the easiest to use. It dries slowly and clear and is useful when working with large images and areas.

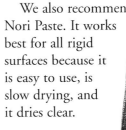

We also recommend Nori Paste. It works best for all rigid surfaces because it is easy to use, is slow drying, and it dries clear.

Crafting beautiful gift tags and cornucopias for ornaments and party favors was a favorite Victorian activity. Gift tags by Jill Miller.

Special-purpose glues include:

Thick tacky white glue. Use this nonrunny glue for heavy, thick papers, trimmings, buttons, fabrics, and beads.

Silicone sealant. This is ideal for hard-to-secure, bulky three-dimensional objects.

Glue gun. These are fun to use and great for trimmings, floral crafts, or three-dimensional objects. The glue dries quickly.

Gluing Technique

If your decoupage will be protected by several coats of finish, you need to have a strong, permanent bond. Cover your worktable with a nonstick surface of wax paper or plastic wrap. Now that your composition is complete and all the images temporarily attached, you are ready to start gluing. Start with the largest, most important pieces first, and fill in with the smaller ones last.

Lift one image a time, remembering to snip off any supporting ladders and remove any temporary adhesive from the cutout. Using a damp glue brush or a polybrush, apply glue generously to cover the *entire* back, spreading evenly from the center out, past all the edges. Press the paper firmly in place with a damp cloth or sponge. Lay a damp disposable cloth (such as a Handi-Wipe) over the glued paper and roll over it with a brayer or a round drinking glass to press out any air bubbles or excess glue. Glue is easiest to remove when wet, so clean off any extra around the edges. If an edge loosens, add a bit more glue under it with a toothpick. A dampened cotton swab works fine for cleaning small interior areas.

Reverse this procedure for gluing under glass. Apply the medium liberally to the back of the glass, in one outlined area, and press the *front* of the print into the glue. Leave the medium to dry clear; just press out the air bubbles, moving them to the nearest edge. Clean off the excess right away, before gluing the next piece.

For a collage where your prints overlap, be sure to glue the underneath pieces first and then the pieces that overlap on top.

For very delicate cutouts or larger pieces of paper, apply the glue to the surface instead of the cutout, then press the paper onto the glue and clean off.

Finishing

Spray sealer is adequate protection for scrapbook pages, greeting cards, and framed artwork. A decorated album cover could be protected with a coat or two of acrylic medium or finish, several coats of spray finish, or a sheet of clear Mylar.

Several layers of clear finish serve to permanently protect your decoupaged object from damage. The more use the piece will get, the more finish coats it needs. Two or three coats are ample for a frame that hangs on the wall, but aim for eight to ten coats on a serving tray. Water-based acrylic polyurethane, an odorless and colorless finish, is an excellent choice. It goes on milky and dries crystal clear to a hard, durable protective coating.

Spray finish protects this album cover.

A matte—not glossy—finish is perfect for this umbrella stand. The elegant print was enlarged to fit.

A tray such as this needs eight or ten coats of finish for protection.

This finish comes in different sheens; choose the one most appropriate for your project. If you've used a higher sheen than you prefer, you can put a coat of matte finish (from the same manufacturer) over the glossy one. Or remove the gloss by rubbing back and forth with #0000 steel wool, then wipe off the residue with a tack cloth.

Read the manufacturer's instructions on the label and always allow plenty of drying time between coats, or the finish might develop cracks later.

Remember, dry to the touch does not mean that the surface is ready for another coat. Let the finish cure more, allow-

ing the moisture to evaporate and the finish to harden. For application of finish, see basic techniques on page 17.

A colorless or white furniture wax applied with a damp soft cloth offers additional protection and gives a lovely patina to your decoupage. Allow a few minutes before buffing with a soft dry cloth.

Glass plates, coasters, and similar items definitely need the protection of a few coats of finish over the entire decorated surface, and please hand wash them—forget the dishwasher.

You've been very patient, we hope, reading and absorbing all this information. Maintain that patience, and your pleasure and pride in your very best and most beautiful work will be your reward. As the writer and artist John Ruskin said, "When love and skill work together, expect a masterpiece."

Protected by ten coats of finish, this keepsake box can be handled safely.

23

Ben just loves to TEND Grandma's garden...

he gets into all the dirt WITH both hands and feet!

I know Gods LOVE is here! Spring 1991

The Gallery

We are delighted to present you with this gallery of Victorian scrap, filled with wonderful images from our collections and from Laura's scrapbook. Let these images from a bygone time inspire you to create.

◆

Clockwise from lower left: This malachite-colored box is simple yet striking. In this scrapbook page by Jill Miller, the addition of trims and other decorative elements recalls the Victorian's approach to design and makes the page a truly personal statement. Knickknacks based on nature, such as this amusing tortoise, were Victorian favorites. At top right, the small green scrapbook is perfect for a single-subject collection of photographs and ephemera. On the hand mirror, light-colored angels are set off by the elegant lapis background. For a quick, rewarding project like the rose coaster, use a single elegant scrap. On the swan tray, the bird was placed slightly off-center for extra drama.

Token of Affection

BIRTHDAY

May circlet of fair blessings sweet
Round your Happy Birthday meet!

CAMBRIDGE

OXFORD

LONDON

EXETER

Albert

BLENHEIM SPANIEL

FOX TERRIER

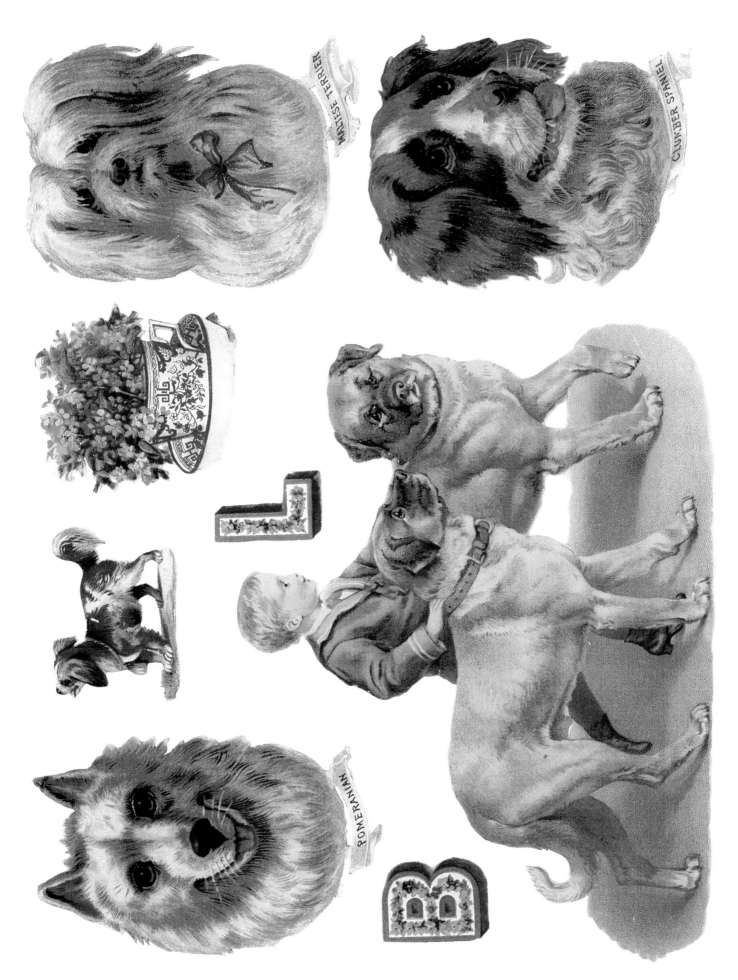

To my
Valentine.

HEARTY WISHES

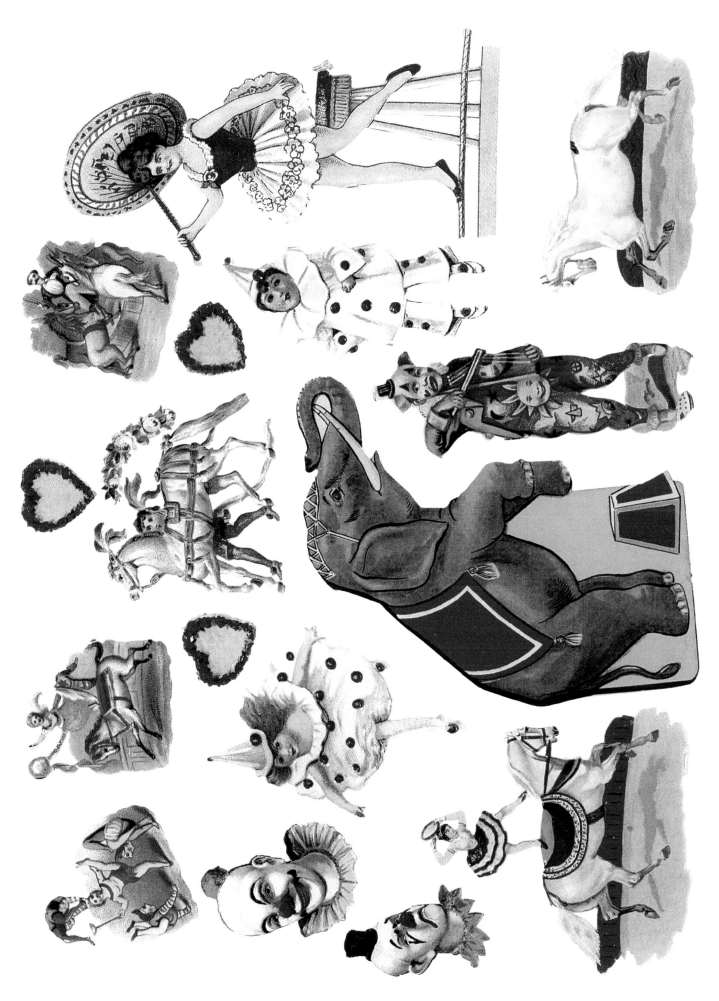

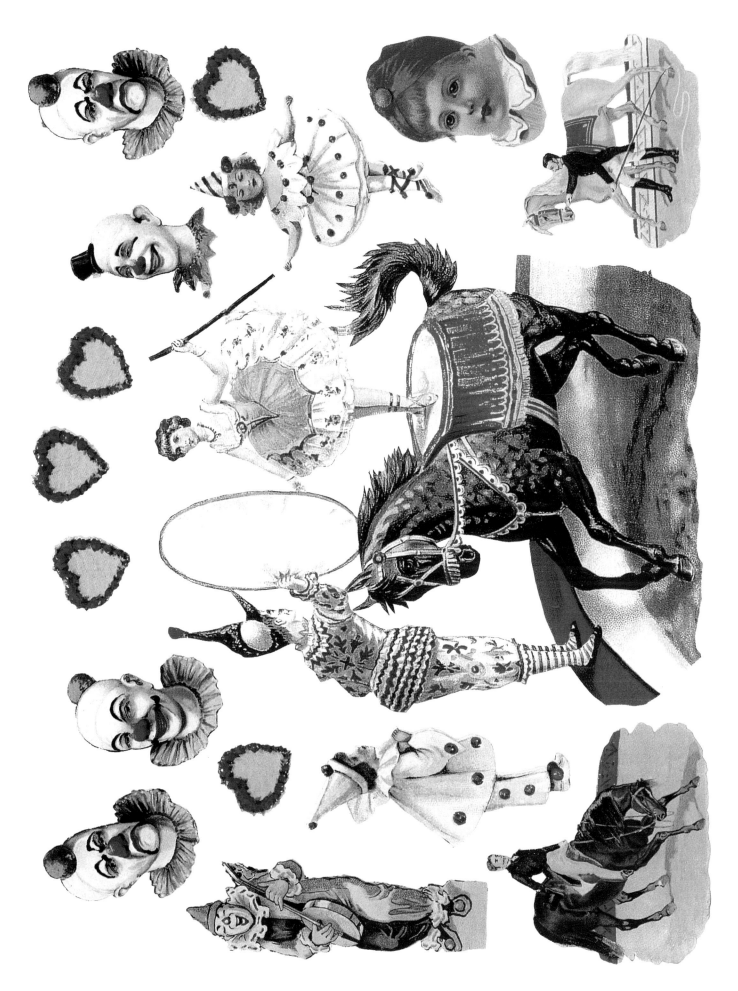

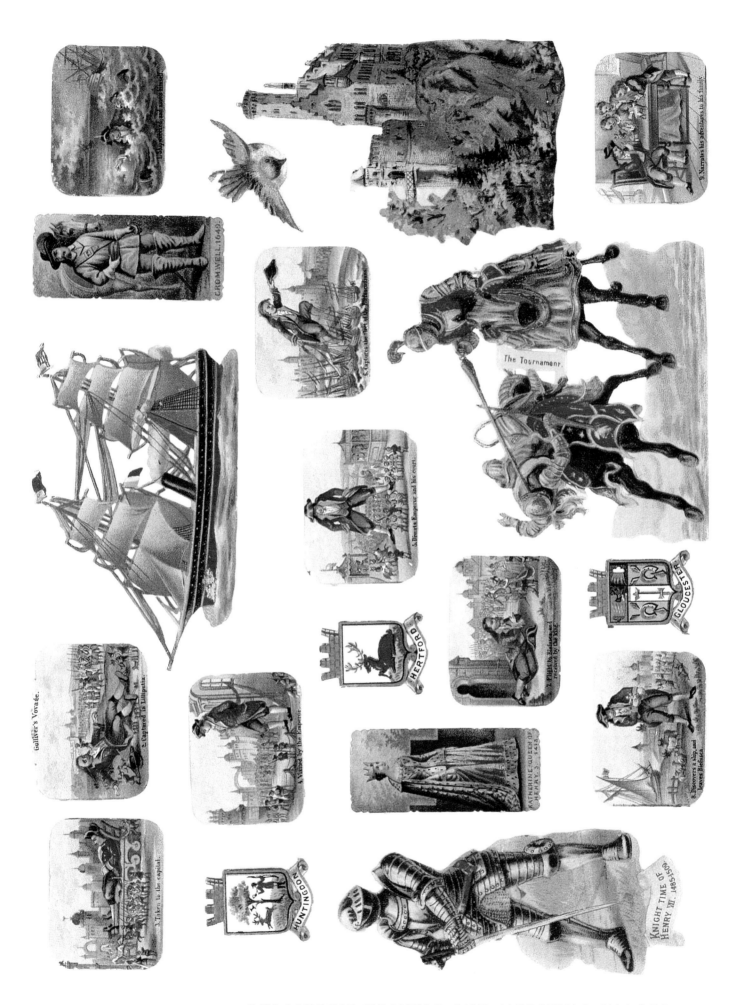

Lear.

Romeo u Julia.

True love.

With loving Greetings

To My Little Sweetheart

Liebe im Herzen lindert alle Schmerzen!

Emanuel Heller
Vienna

To One I Fondly Love

My dear Sweetheart

Rest in the Lord, and wait patiently for Him. *Psa. 37.7.*

My presence
shall go with thee and I will give thee rest. *Ex. 33.14.*

Love One Another.

Jolly Christmas.

A happy New Year

Happy New Year!

Resources

Listed below are the manufacturers and suppliers for some of the materials used in this book. The manufacturers sell their products exclusively to art supply and crafts retailers, which are a consumer's most dependable source for paper crafting and decoupage supplies. Your local retailer can advise you on purchases and can order a product for you if they don't have it in stock. If you can't find a store in your area that carries a particular item or will accept a request for an order, or if you need special assistance, a manufacturer can direct you to the retailer nearest you that carries their products and will try to answer any technical questions you might have. When purchasing hard-to-find or specialized materials, it's best to deal with specialized mail order and Internet sources.

Manufacturers

Plaid Enterprises
3225 Westech Drive
Norcross, GA 30092
(800) 329-8673
Paints, finishes, and kits.

Yasutomo
490 Eccles Avenue
South San Francisco, CA 94080
(800) 262-6454
The source for Nori paste.

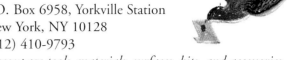

Mail-Order Resources

Adventures in Crafts Studio
P.O. Box 6958, Yorkville Station
New York, NY 10128
(212) 410-9793
Decoupage tools, materials, surfaces, kits, and accessories.

D. Blümchen and Company, Inc.
P.O. Box 1210 D
Ridgewood, NJ 07451
(866) 653-9627
Ornaments, decorations, and a large assortment of gold-embossed paper braid and trim.

Tinsel Trading Co.
47 West 38th St.
New York, NY 10018
(212) 730-1030
Vintage and reproduction, decorative ribbons, tassels, fringe, cording, and gold-embossed paper braid and trim.

Internet Resources

Two of our favorites are scrapalbum.com, a personal website compiled by scrap admirer Malcolm Warrington, and ephemerasociety.org, the website of the Ephemera Society of America. Both list many links for additional information about scrap.

Further Reading

Davis, Dee. *Decoupage: Paper Cutouts for Decoration and Pleasure.* London: Thames and Hudson, 2000.

Davis, Dee, and Cooper, Gail B. *The Decoupage Gallery: A Collection of Over 450 Color and 550 Black and White Design Motifs.* New York: Watson-Guptill Publications, 2001.

Grotz, George. *The Furniture Doctor: A Guide to the Care, Repair and Refinishing of Furniture.* New York: Doubleday, 1989.

Leland, Nita, and Williams, Virginia L. *Creative Collage Techniques.* Cincinnati: North Light Books, 1994.

Pearce, Amanda. *The Crafters' Complete Guide to Collage.* New York: Watson-Guptill Publications, 1997.

Miller, Jill. *Special-Effects Scrapbooking: Creative Techniques for Scrapbookers at All Levels.* New York: Watson-Guptill Publications, 2003.

Index